YOU ARE HER

Also by Linda France

POETRY
Acts of Love (Echo Room Press), 1990
Red (Bloodaxe Books), 1992
The Gentleness of the Very Tall (Bloodaxe), 1994
Storyville (Bloodaxe), 1997
The Simultaneous Dress (Bloodaxe), 2002
Aerogramme (Talking Pen), 2003
wild (Sand Press), 2003
The Toast of the Kit Cat Club (Bloodaxe), 2005
The Moon & Flowers (Queen's Hall Arts), 2008
book of days (Smokestack Books), 2009

ANTHOLOGIES
Sixty Women Poets (editor, Bloodaxe Books),1993
Sauce (editor, Bloodaxe Books), The Poetry Virgins, 1995

TRANSLATIONS
A Balkan Exchange (Arc Publications), 2007

PLAYS
Diamonds in your Pockets, for Théâtre sans Frontières, 1997
I am Frida Kahlo, for Cloud Nine Theatre Company, 2003

YOU ARE HER
Linda France

PUBLICATIONS
2010

Published by Arc Publications
Nanholme Mill, Shaw Wood Road
Todmorden OL14 6DA, UK
www.arcpublications.co.uk

Copyright © Linda France 2010
Design by Tony Ward
Printed in Great Britain by the
MPG Book Group, Bodmin & King's Lynn

978 1906570 55 2 pbk
978 1906570 56 9 hbk

ACKNOWLEDGEMENTS:
Poems have previously appeared in
*The Ropes, Storyville, Mslexia, Stand, Tomorrow's Moon,
Gift – A Chapbook for Seamus Heaney,
The Heart as Origami, Blinking Eye,*
Yorkshire Open Poetry Competition,
Writing on the Wall, Tate etc, Poetry Review,
Culture North East, *Stripe,* Tweed Rivers Project,
*Diamond Twig, Poems Deep and Dangerous,
The Verb, The Simultaneous Dress, The Rialto,
Dhamma Moon, Other Poetry.*

With thanks to Kim Lewis, Nick Owen, Ajahn
Abhinando, and John Clarke, Tony Ward and
Angela Jarman, editors at Arc.

The cover photograph is the gate into the
walking meditation garden at Harnham Buddhist
Monastery, taken by Linda France.

Supported by
ARTS COUNCIL
ENGLAND

Editor for the UK and Ireland: John W Clarke

For Rufus and Nathaniel

CONTENTS

HERE

HER

We are all of us strange little quilts,
patches of father-tone in some of our tissues,
shades of our mother in others… It is the woman who is
the greater mosaic, a patchwork of her past…
We are more motley by far than our brothers.

NATALIE ANGIER, 'Woman: An Intimate Geography'

DYING IN MY SLEEP

When I woke up I was dead;
the memory of how it happened
like a lift shaft on the outside
of the high-rise of my body.

The penthouse was a car smashed
apart, a shock of smoke
and metal and I was flying
over tarmac, a broken white line.

Halfway down was a man
at the wheel, not looking
where he was going, in love
with all the traffic, speed.

Ground floor was knowing
I was dead and this is what
it feels like: utterly empty,
wide open. And still not over.

In the basement I find
a woman in the wing mirror
who sees me, offers me
a lift in her vehicle of black light.

YES

Like a baby bird in the nest,
I was fed the lie Mother knows best.

Daddy had some persuasion too.
I'd do whatever he wanted me to.

When I'd learned more than they both knew,
I looked to my teachers for what was true.

Their favourite words were *Don't* and *No,*
so how could I tell which way to go?

I asked friends and enemies, loved and loathed.
Not one shed light on the right road.

That task was mine and mine alone,
a skill I was never taught how to hone.

Now I practise *Yes, Do* and *Try.*
Sometimes I fall, but sometimes I can fly.

WAITING WITH MY YELLOW DOG

The woman who sleeps all day
makes origami birds
out of toffee wrappers.

Her neighbour's zimmer
kicks its rubber hooves, dreaming
of gentle jockeys with white hair.

My ears, powerful as whelks,
practise listening moistly,
like a slug, trailing silver.

I cool the air in the tomb
of my lips with glyphs of gold,
mistrals whispering at the doors,

windows hooked with flamingo beaks.
A yellow dog sits at my side,
drinking all my sins. We are twins,

nameless, faithful, Siamese.
Night surrenders into day
with the charm of real birds

in an imaginary garden,
fine as the cracks in my bones.
Hot flanks twitching, my bed hacks

towards dawn. The starched sheets
stripe me sore in the saddle.
The nurses' shoes sing me

a lullaby in morse;
hands stroke me like owls, dapple
me like mares, fluff my pillows

into the bellies of bears.
All night long I lie there
waiting for my hair to turn white.

AFTER

Because no one taught her
she had to be careful who she told her
despair to, she found out on her
own and she found out deeper
she found out wider
the heart of her
smashed against the wall behind her.

Listen to her
now counting her
skins, the ones she lost, her
nearest and dearest, those left her
the new ones she found under
what she thought was all so no wonder
she doesn't know what's her.

YOU DON'T KNOW WHAT LOVE IS

Count the years it went into hiding and you
walked down a long road in a body you

couldn't call your own. Every time you
looked all you could see was bone. You

swallowed a memory of milk and, waking, you
felt no thirst. In a dry country, you

were never hungry. Your thoughts were blue. You
collected them like jewels, the only family you

owned. What saved you from desert, what brought you
through was the cadence of music not being played. You

had to find it on your own. It was time for you
to fall slowly into those open spaces you

were afraid of, where you couldn't let go. You
let go and tunnelled through the tight dark you

knew would deliver you into that tune you
couldn't hear, those chords pulsing just for you.

THUNDERTOWN

The only thing we're sure of is the sky –
shades of black over rooftops angled

like lightning spikes. The roads are closed.
Rain practises the monsoon as if it were a dance step.

The aspens are begging for it, glossy and winking.
We watch the lights going on and off –

a nervous tic, side effect of the medication
we've been swallowing for years. Is it us

or the weather that's grown into this
viking skin, slinging hammers at the day

like a tantrumming child throwing toys
out of its cot? What isn't clap or roar

or stamping foot settles into a low thrum,
the tinnitus of a mind with too much to say

for itself. Gulls gather on the sandbanks
of the city's murky river too panicked to fly away.

We long for cover, look at each other
as if for the first time, as if we might need

a hand to hold, a body to huddle against
in the static; share our certain illumination.

Her Hands. A Phone Box in Andalucia.
Paper Scissors Stone. A Clock for Seeing.
The Squeeze. What Things Look Like When They're Not There.

Notting Hill, Varanasi. A Prayer.
Goody Two Shoes. Patience. The Gladdening.
When Light Falls. The Left-Handed Piano.

His Artichoke Heart. The Knucklebone Floor.
Reading Material. Then the Haunting.
What To Do About The Mice. Star Fruit. May.

Stone Fruit. Fish. A Spell to Dissolve Desire.
Driving in the Dark. Blue Yodelling.
Jet. The Life Cycle of the Dragonfly.

Swedish for Luck. The White Room. War Weather.
All Her Geese Were Swans. New Planet. Unsung.
Breathing in Colour. Sumatran Tiger.
Lies I Have Told. Glory Hole. Heart Sutra.

WHAT THE BEAM SAID

There was never enough air;
always the possibility of falling.

My decisive horizontal exhaled
its polished grain between them.

They would lose each other slowly
while they were sleeping.

Skins thicker, eyes blinder.
Dreams of felled trees – Beech,

Norwegian Spruce – they wouldn't mention.
Sawdust on the pillows.

Soundless, I axis east-west, slice
the empty space in two.

Not forgetting that word. *We.*
Like wood. How soft it is. How hard.

THE BREAK

If you're lucky there will always be
a white horse called Pandora who'll rear
and throw you so you can't get up and walk

away. Where did you think you were going?
The circus trick's not covering your eyes
when Pandora cries *Look! Can't you see*

you're in danger? Still you try, studying
so hard how to mend one thing, no inkling
of what else might be broken. You carry

your fractures around like a bad smell
you imagine is coming from the rooms
you walk through, the people you talk to.

Everything tastes sour on your tongue,
and you lose your appetite. Easy
to fall from there to where all of you

is aching. Until at last you crack open
like an egg, spilling the gold you must lay out
and count, your wound's treasure. Only here,

your shell smashed, can the healing start;
like a myth about horses, the print
of hooves in sand. And you see nothing

is what you think it is; nothing to do
with you and what you know. It hurts
and will always hurt; and you're utterly changed

by it. And it's just this: steady
as the breath that breathes you, that only needs
you to be there, tall in the saddle.

VERTEBRA

If this is bone, I can't believe it's what I'm made of.
It could be carved out of ivory, a squat angel;
some vestiges of flesh, as if once it flavoured soup.

I hesitate to touch its greasy roughness, smelling
of something lost, something buried deep inside.
Two small holes tell me nothing of what made them.

I wonder if anyone will hold mine in the palm
of their hand, the one with a crack in its left wing
that unlocked all the hurt in me and took years

of stillness to heal. I'm trying to imagine what a scar
looks like in bone – maybe a white landscape
with a gentle ridge a person could learn to walk again along.

FRIDA KAHLO'S CORSET

It's a garden of stars.
A screaming skull.
Hammer and sickle.
It locks her in.

Two of her paint
it, mirror angled
beneath her breasts.
She lies flat, rests.

It's a plaster vase
I arrange the stem
of myself in; it drinks
sweat, my sins.

There's no escape
in its hollow trunk,
a spineless tree,
staring out at sky.

KNITBONE

Don't be fooled by my soft folds.
I feed the earth and fix bones.
My tuberous roots, hidden,
as all the best things are,
   mend what is broken:
   the cue of all my names
for curing, soothing what is sore,
unsundering. If you know
   what you need, why ignore
   the remedy? Let me bring my way
with bones to all your blindness.
Look again at my pleated creams:
   See how I am bell and lantern.
   Breathe in the smell of morning rain.

THE BURNING HOUSE

When a single thought recurring caught
like paper under magnified sunlight,

it didn't take long till flames licked their lips
and devoured windowsill, curtains, chair;

the whole room blackening into one
enormous grate. The towers of books were tinder,

tumbling into clips from the end of the world;
all the words incinerated till nothing

was left of Babel but grey flakes
of lost imaginings. The stairs turned

into the scales of an orange dragon
and the chimney roared. Last to go was the bed,

its mattress resisting the familiar heat,
proud of its memory of metaphor,

its love for play. In the end, even it was powerless.
By morning all that remained were shadows,

coils of wire. This is what I came home to;
for the first time felt air open through me, pure

as the water that couldn't put the fire out,
strong as the earth deep in my bones.

THE GOOSE AND THE BOTTLE

There is a goose inside a bottle.
There is a bottle with a goose inside.
How does the goose get out of the bottle?
How does the goose stay alive?
How does the bottle stay unbroken?
Where is the goose? Where is the bottle?
You are the goose. You are the bottle.
You are the goose inside the bottle.
Close your eyes: the goose is inside the bottle.
Say it: the goose is out of the bottle.
Believe it: the bottle is not broken, the goose alive.
Open your eyes: the goose is out of the bottle.
There is the goose. There is the bottle.
You have become the goose out of the bottle.
You are not broken. You are alive.

MOONSHINE

Even in the middle of saying it
I know the argument my lips
are trying to convince themselves of –
and you, of course – is fragile
as a web strung with dew,
jewel for just one morning,
air's own fibres made visible.

Not to mention the autopsy
of words and sentences – laying
them out on the slab of my head,
picking them over for evidence
of violence, pretence, some weakness
I take out of the dark to make
sure I'm not sure about.

The brightest knowing happens
in silence, alone, those empty
spaces where I can notice how
things begin and bring their own
ending: the same way I watch
the coming and going of the moon,
enchanted by borrowed light.

CORONA

You were the ring around my moon,
light smudged into an absence

of colour, soft as the bloom
around someone sleeping, opposite of iris.

What you breathed into me was the other
side of shadow, oil marbling

a puddle. I called you my dark brother,
the only one who could free the bubbles

beneath my craters, gentle the cold bed
of my arid sea. You were my edge,

my naked eye, where my eclipsed heart led,
high and dry, the best of me.

WHAT LOVE IS LIKE IN WINTER

Show me the place where your collar grazes
your neck: thick wool – dove grey, loose knit –
haloes skin, half-buried, flawed, tender.

It is a few inches of shadows,
the warm nest of your voice, your swallow,
the small room where all your geese are cooked.

You pluck the feathers of touch and go,
always on the point now of vanishing
like snow melting overnight, berries
bitten from the branch on the wing.

The attic of your beautiful throat
is laced with owl and cobweb. Night sings north,
the need of winter. Look up and know
what will become of us is stars.

THE CHANGE

She carries it around like a geek's secret
that leaks out when least expected, crackling

on contact with what plusses hang in the air.
Anything but still, it dazzles and fries her

with the friction of its intent. Every strand
of hair heading north, making a dalek bid

for freedom, her ticking halo belongs
to someone else, a ragamuffin sprite

who gets up to no good; so charged she clings
to walls and sends folk away pink and tingling.

Hers is loud music bled from high-strung
Fenders, satanic lyrics played backwards, for kicks.

She'd be better off tripping the switch, not
plugging into her per capita power,

its static discharge, one shock after another.
Only sparks after all, brief as lightning.

CAVE PAINTING

My skin is wrinkling, growing ochreish;
a whiff of peat rising from the tundra
between my toes. Natural pigments
speckle palmprint, dot scar and mole.

After my bath I trace the shapes
of buffalo, deer, galloping foal;
dry the tribe's prizes
in my cracks – tarsal, oxter, jaw.

That wildness spiralled in my hair
echoes mane, backbone, tail:
not a single strand falling
from the same time's fold.

Certain crannies, my skeleton
is starting to show. In others
it's buried beneath an overhang
of freckle and pucker, lichen-glow.

Sable-brushed, chiselled, smudged,
my body is a palimpsest of stone,
settling back into the earth
she came from thousands of years ago.

RECONSTRUCTION

Everything that's left looks like something else –
head, a rusty bucket, stoved in where
the axe hit; ears like dried fungi; skin
like tanned hide, bleached fig; the bowl
of your chest. A cord round your neck, fur band
holding the flesh and bone of your arm together,
as if you were nothing but trussed meat.

Your body's fallen into metaphor – food
and the vessels it rests in – a last communion.

The only hinge between our worlds
is the evidence of your last meal –
a griddle cake baked from quern-ground wheat,
a sprinkling of barley, the yellow dust
of mistletoe pollen; traces of whipworm
still clinging to your gut. The journey
sustained by what passed your lips can't be seen,

like time itself, and what survives; only
tasted – the sacrifice and the healing.

THE LOVE POTION OF POLEMIOS

*

He wouldn't tell me what was in it.
It tasted of river, a tang of trout
with a trickle of heat under it,
wine to help it slip down gently.
It slipped down gently as a willow
                    coming into leaf.

*

I dreamt of gloves and shoes, the finest hide,
a second skin. Waking up was like dancing.
The sun lifted the sleep out of my hair
and I was up with the squirrels. Naked
as a baby. Hungry as a slave. Eyes
                    dry as kindling.

*

The first time I saw him I was a bird,
all feathers and song. From up there
on the balcony I saw the sun
turn his hair to bronze as he walked.
I lost all power of flight. My face burned.
Couldn't tell if the heat was his or mine.
He didn't look up. I swear if he did
                    I would have gone blind.

*

Crowned and tawny, my lion heart.
Something gold about his eyes. He looks at me
slowly and I glisten. Makes me wait
till the sun is an arrow in the sky.
The best omen. He is the emperor
of amber, and I am a fly
            locked in yellow light.

*

He invented magnetism. Science
was on his side. He brings me a bowl
of April, its lip so curved and gentle,
I catch fire. It takes an hour to get used
to the dazzle. We both powder into ash,
            thinking of nothing but water.

*

The claw of morning. His early hungry rays.
Water and wine. A craving for trout.

BURDENED CHILDREN

All the pieces of the world they carry,
legs buckling with the weight of memory –
but still they walk together in the same
direction, eyes on a horizon
that might keep from vanishing if they can
only leave the squares that have grown on
the rough angles of their shoulders, bones
exposed, behind them on that road where
the wind blows. How many catastrophes
must a child be burdened by while the rest
of us reconcile the distance between
what we want and where we've been, gather
hand, heart and eye by degrees into light
enough to let conscience lift the weather?

Paul Klee 1930

FALLING

When he told me about the guillemots
and kittiwakes, how their numbers
are falling, how he'd watched them roost
on cliffs ever since he was a child,
he lifted his hand over his eyes
and cried.
          I heard the attic room swell
with the ache and crack of calling birds,
wings in flight beating walls to dust,
his whole house falling into the Dene,
so I could see what it is that's left
when everything you love is lost.

STAGSHAW FAIR

If there's a spectre in the air, it's hard
to find in the mizzle smudging the line
between land and sky and the Blackface herd
that scatters as I swing past the footpath sign.

I know this place, these roads, like my own bones
and also love its secrets. I've walked
the fair, the north, inside myself. Its stones
are fallen walls, markers where the way forked.

A constellation of returning birds
offers itself as puzzle more than omen.
Where do we think we live? I sift the words
in layers. *Who with?* Gorse. Redwing. Roman.

Whether we go to the fair, or we don't,
won't we all come home pockets full of ghosts?

SORROW

Every morning at five I'm woken
by thuds and taps at the window.
I tune them out, tunnelling under
white cotton dark.
                    After a week
of early alarms, I get up
to find myself face to face
with a magpie, caught mid-peck,
trying to steal the silver;

the glint of candlestick and chimes
all it takes to fire his desire,
deny the fact of glass.
                    I cover
the shine with a cloth as if
it were a sleeping bird, close
the curtains and return to bed,
unable to settle for thinking about
all the things I've ever wanted.

YOU

For although we are accustomed to separate nature and human perception into two realms, they are, in fact, indivisible. Before it can ever be a repose for the senses, landscape is the work of the mind. Its scenery is built up as much from strata of memory as from layers of rock.

Simon Schama, 'Landscape and Memory'

BIOGRAPHY

If you were to stitch a suit
to bring a man back to life,
it would look like this. Close
your eyes and imagine it:
felt – wholemeal fibres pressed
together; a suggestion of animal
seeking its home, rat hair, rabbit pelt.
No fastenings. Stout lapels
and slit cuffs; a little placket
for the fly. Let two pockets flap
like letterboxes; post a single pocket
where the heart will rest.

It asks to be stroked but the pattern
does not permit it. Only the one
who sews it can know what
this two-piece feels like inside –
how wool warms and creases,
moulds itself to the body's stretch
and ease, its vulnerable seams,
wrap of soft sleeves – more naked
in his surrender to the felt touch
than barest skin or brightest hope.

BIRTHPLACE

I want to breathe you in like a picture
under my skin. I want to see your face
before you were born when all you were

was capability. I want to say I've summoned
you. But it's a car park now the house
where you grew up and your father died.

In the café Doris Day is singing
The future's not ours to see as smoke blows
a ghost over the fields to Cambo.

CAPABILITY

For fourteen years I've duelled with this garden,
caught between what is impossible
and its simple, perfect capability.
The fence is no match for cattle and sheep
who believe my grass is greener despite
the industrious tunnelling, earthworks
of rabbits and moles, the highs and lows
of seven-hundred-foot weather. Together
we've lost countless summers.
                                    This September,
berries heavy on the rowan tree,
dragonflies skimming the pond, rye and fescue
go back to seed, dry to hay, gathering
for home like the swallows busy circling.
Whatever I do with mower or trowel,
nothing will stop the world falling further
into its own. My body wants to call it
humility, hands open enough to take
and hold.
            On the other side of the fence,
my mind convinces itself, nothing's changed –
windburnt fell, far hills tinged blue in the glass
of sky, the city that glitters like flowers
in the east come nightfall: all as much
my garden as this small quarter-acre
I struggle to tame, the wild creeping
closer on outstretched claws every second,
bearing what seems possible, and more.

THE LINE OF BEAUTY

It's a surprise to hear Harewood chiming
with 'heart-wood' not 'hare-wood' and to trace
the line of beauty Lancelot Brown drew
from his native north – those echoes of hill

and burn, the sky-blue veneer dancing
on dark water. A single copper beech
on the open lawn inches the eye towards
a gap in the treeline, Almscliffe Crags

on the far horizon. The ear follows
calling birds to a waterfall's spitting gush;
everything redolent of natural charms
just natural enough not to frighten us.

No need to fear what's lurking in the woods.
It's brash on banners, in print – Drive-in Movie
(*Dirty Dancing*), Chinese State Circus,
Girls Aloud. We need him now, Lancelot Brown,
his love of beauty, his way with lines.

BROWNIFICATION

As if the landscape were a page
in a book, you arrange it
word by word, weighing
every inflexion, the flow
of syntax, the halts of punctuation –
imagine an elm in summer
as a comma; a colon, say,
for this curving turn in gravel;
the soothing parenthesis of water.

Your place-making is, you confess,
grammatical: your pragmatic genius
patterning what a wild eye sees,
how the prospect might lift
a hopeless heart heavenward;
the site, your rivals suggest,
for your next project –
always scope for progress,
one full stop before another.

NATURE LESSONS

Stalking blue-jewelled slow-worms, quick ruby hips,
I'd spot the soft-boiled yellow of kingcup and celandine,
names I'd learnt from the cards in our PG Tips;

whole days decanting tadpoles or sticklebacks
into smuggled jars, mud making moons under
my fingernails, plastic sandals squelching like ducks.

'Down the lane' and 'behind the railway line'
are continents lost to me – and, forty years on, the world –
where I learnt what earth was for, what grew where,

how time could disappear, the way trees smelled,
dripping with diamonds, after rain; the blessing
of it never judging, sweet as cobnuts nestled in velvet.

It was safe to run wild as the tangled brambles
and coconut gorse that clawed my calves and arms
into a tracery of scars, stinging nettles' morse code.

With nothing there asking to be understood,
my natural curiosity was fearless and golden,
free to do whatever it could – clamber, paddle, look.

Only night and hunger drove me home, behind
closed doors, where we all knew what would happen
next and everyone's face was empty.

HEALTH & PLENTY

What if *Health* and *Plenty* were two sphinxes
guarding the gates of all our houses?

A lion's heart in a woman's breast is
at home with life and death, the riddles

posed by being human, wanting what's best
for our children: the ground beneath their feet,

not just safe but beautiful, and fertile.
Summon her wise serpent's tail, agile,

endless, her legendary wings, tranquil
on pillar and step. Let *Peace* and *Goodwill*

be forged from iron to crown our rooftops,
grace the land across our timid thresholds.

CASCADE

I dreamt I offered you all
the waterfalls of Europe
in a samovar wrought
from silver. When you lifted
the lid, we were deafened
by them roaring, as if all
the wars declared between then
and now on foreign soil
were raging at once – sticks
and stones, what everyone wants –
there on your lap; the worsted
of your travelling breeches
worn thin with wrangling;
the opposite of enlightenment.

PSYCHE LEANS TOWARDS LOVE

Her skin marble, chilled,
Psyche carries a lamp – not to warm her
but to shed some light on the one
who shares her bed when night falls
and rests on her eyes, ears full of listening.
She grips a dagger, just in case.

He and whatever way lies ahead
are nameless, invisible, moth-palled,
until she can shine her own light, leaning
towards all the unfathomable dark.

Where she longs to find herself is also
how she needs to proceed – those small
careful steps she must take towards
what she knows now is Love; giving
herself to every obstacle, regardless
of the burden of the necessary tasks,

ineluctable as dawn, what she will uncover
there – home, all, its willing wings.

THREE LOOKS AT A LAKE

Word has it the lake and the land it lightens
was unfinished, begun in a flurry
then abandoned through lack of money,
distrust of the estate's prodigal son,
got above himself, supping with viscounts
and lords. Nothing irks those who stay at home
more than the maverick's return, spinning
tales by the yard and his pockets straining.

Call the lake a mirror and stand north of it
below the knoll: here it's split in two –
humble ponds for geese and swans; the hill
rising behind it up to Codger's Fort.

From there, as if by magic, the lake
vanishes behind a veil of horizon.

Walk down to the old boathouse,
its ruined walls, and see how silver snakes
into river, winding between banks,
out of sight, and the broad arms of sycamore.

Every view is another facet
of the land's lending, all it offers
those with eyes to see. Not unlike the man
who designed it – and all of us, showing
our different faces to the world
as the weather changes and long days close
their shutters and light their fires: seeing
and being seen, ice and ice melting.

ON GOING TO A LECTURE ON CAPABILITY BROWN CALLED 'COPYING NATURE'

Two hundred and ninety years after
your birth, I'm driving through snow
falling so thick it's impossible to tell
what time of day it is or where this
country road begins, where it might end;
white as the paper you sketched your plans on,

getting whiter by the mile. I hold my breath.

The three radiators in the Village Hall
aren't up to the cocoon of snow it's wrapped in.
For one hour twenty people in scarves and hats
think about repoussoir and the picturesque,
what we'd see if we were bold enough – like you –
to uproot everything we don't need,

gaining the depth that would fill its absence.

Back in the car, I hold onto the slipping wheel
to stop myself falling and losing my edges –
like all your landscapes erased
by tarmac and railway, time and weather.

LAST DAY

It's a lucky man who's murdered
returning from church, the light
of prayer and tallow still bright
and burning somewhere deep inside.

Zealous reivers creep behind
him and with daggers and swords
slice him into pieces to find
it – but only blood on their hands.

It's butcher's work dividing
the dripping meat between the bags
on his saddle and, whacking her flanks,
sending his horse back home, steaming.

None of us can know how or when
our death will happen – till then
we must make our own devotions.

HERE

In bullfighting there's a place in the bullring where the bull feels safe. If he can reach this place he stops running and can gather his full strength. He's no longer afraid. From the point of view of the matador he becomes dangerous and this place in the ring is different for every bull.

It is the job of the matador to be sure that the bull does not have time to occupy this place of wholeness. This safe place is called the querencia in bullfighting.

And for human beings there is also such a place; for when a person finds their querencia, in full view of the matador they're calm and steady, wise. They've gathered their strength around them and the silence of that moment is more secure than any hiding place.

JACK KORNFIELD

JOY

Two magpies loiter, wing to wing, at the lip
of the pond; dip big bills into its dark bowl.

A patina of cobalt flashes behind bellies, fat
and soft as cream. There is chattering

and nodding. Later, through the gate,
over the glade of cottongrass, they're still

together, slicing the sky in two; spelling
it out – inky feathers, skin and bone.

GULLS

How a scarf shaken out
ripples, folds around itself
and whatever air it finds,
the gulls are flocking
over the Tyne.
How, as dusk falls, they know
it's time to fly together,
knit their flickering stitches,
white against darkening sky.
After a day of solitary soaring,
suddenly they are tribe.
How all things become more
than they are
alongside another.
How driving home
to an empty house
triggers my longing
for edge and threshold,
the possibility of flight,
a scarf of shared air.

TWO RIVERS

Water is good for all living things. It flows without thinking
where it is going.

Tao Te Ching

Tweed said to the Till
What gars ye rin sae still?
Till said to Tweed
Though ye rin wi' speed
And I rin slow
Yet where ye droon yin man I droon twa.

Traditional Verse

BOWMONT WATER

If there is a gateway,

there must also be a threshold,

a border to tread between two worlds.

There is in and out. There is open and closed.

You are a gypsy. You are not a gypsy.

Keep walking. Even if you don't know where

you are going, keep on walking.

You are climbing Venchen Hill, looking for

the Virtue Well. You want to make a wish.

You want its holy water to soothe your thirst.

The gorse is growing wild, the trees

have lost their way. Even the walls

are falling. You cannot find the well.

Keep walking.

There is a lake. It drowns trees.
A grey ellipse, it is home for birds
that swim out of their element – moorhens,
gulls, a family of swans. This is valley,
where earth accepts the fact of water.
It cools you with its whisper of agate, jasper.
Keep on walking.

RIVER TILL

You thought the brass said 'To the *Brace*
of Both Nations', where King James fell;
the book tells you '*Brave*'. You don't know
what made the scars in the side of Twizel Bridge,
what march, what battle; only read
the beauty of lichen, freedom of sycamore wings.
Keep on walking.

This is the place where two rivers meet,
the Till and the Tweed. It is a long Y,
a beginningless, endless question you'll ask
the Himalayan Balsam's purple mirror.
This side is England; the other Scotland.
Can't go forward, can't go back, can't stay still.
Keep walking.

Past the mill at Etal, there's a broken
footbridge. Wooden steps rise into nowhere,
can't cross the river. A blistered sign still warns
no more than two people must walk it
at once. The sound of the water spilling
over the weir rinses your ears.
Keep on walking.

There is more pleasure in bridges than gateways.
Where one element joins another, it doesn't add up
to two. You count them on your fingers:
earth, water, air; today, yesterday, tomorrow;
Bowmont, Till, Tweed. Always more
than you think there is. Keep walking,
friend, there are three of us, and we are ocean.

WILDLING

As hard to imagine a Spring without
daffodils as to look at the world
and not see your face in it. I don't want
to admit either are possible

walking along this path – beech mast crunchy
underfoot, ants in heaps of muscovado,
what might be a redstart on the horizon –

then kneeling in front of these daffodils,
soft as light, strong as woodland quiet,
small cups of sun full of the taste of earth.

If I told you, ground and mixed with barley meal,
they could heal wounds, would you look at me
from wherever you are like an echo –
wild and blowing and gold and open?

for Julia Darling (1956 - 2005)

SADNESS AS BILLY'S LEEKS FAIL TO WIN POSTHUMOUS PRIZE

PE teacher weds rugby player.
Cat vendetta, claims owner.
Police saw man in ski mask run from store.
Pair went too far. Youth swore.

Rottweiler killed goat. Car ran into horse.
Hanging baskets repaired. New bins sought.
Tools taken. Bucket stolen.
Car wrecks goal posts. Car wasn't stolen.

Beer bottle hit car. Tax disc out of date.
Landlady fined for pub's slate.
Karaoke complaints. House could be school.
Cow falls into swimming pool.

Firemen start fire. Vicar joins sewage gang.
Angry man broke window of caravan.
Library under attack. Police van stoned.
More police wanted. Enough post boxes.

MY MOTHER'S LEEK PUDDING

My mother did it in secret in our kitchen,
wreathed in vapours of steam and grease.
The yellow Venetian blinds lowered their eyes.
She did it quickly as if to get it over with,
as if it was nothing, an invisible art.
And because she hated cooking. Because
she hated eating. That thing you did
between cigarettes; hard to swallow.
Atora, Atora, Atora the packet whispered.
When I looked again it was all puff
and billow, a glassy sheen on the soft mound,
the sweet fragrance of leeks, my mother's glasses

all misted up.

So now I'm having trouble letting my hands
do what they have to without me getting
in the way, muttering *vegetarian, low fat,*
and making a fist of it. My kitchen's as small
as hers but there's room enough for her
to come back and show me how to sift the flour
and butter the dish, how to wrap the dough
round the green treasure of the leeks
like a white quilt, plump it up like pillows;
for us to work out together the best way
to steam it with something like love. Invisible
till it's risen and on the table to feed you.

WEATHER VANE

Once it seemed as if my parents
were only weather but now I see
they were also the spinning vane to tell it by.

My father's the proud vertical,
a steel arrow of love and grief
he let fall in my direction

and I carry in my spine's doubts
and shadows. His gift was tears,
a knack for precipitation.

My mother's body is the horizontal
that climbs and hides, east to west.
Opposite her husband in every way,

she taught me contradiction –
given space and silence – is equatorial,
an imaginary line between hearts.

Together they blew hot and cold, passing
chill and fever on to me to heal;
old wounds, torn in the winds

of war and what it was to be poor
with no words of their own
to tell it by, our family's weather.

TARA

See how her eyes are like gulls, gliding
across the white mist of her face.
Or whales swimming in the deep of it.
So liquid is her skin, her hair hesitates
to begin. Her nose studies the curled petals
of her tiny lips and decides to name
everything *lotus* and *lily* and *open*.

What can you do with a woman like that
but lay your head in her lap and breathe
the heat from her belly, the *in*, the *out* of it?
Bring her the courage of your sadness
because that's all you have left and let
the calm weight of her hand soothe you,
her total absence of drama and façade.

The map around your sternum you try to keep fixed
she melts, matching you breath for breath.
You are molten gold, older than angel hair.
You've lost all your edges. Which one
of you lifts up her head? Borrow her crown,
those flames. Your neck will be a column of air.
Wish all the people wisdom, wish them well.

BORROWING A GRANDMOTHER

Even though she's iron, with studs for eyes,
I choose this one, hang her likeness, full-size,
on the sitting room wall. She'll keep vigil
as I copperplate my inventory
of imaginary uncles, heirlooms
bequeathed by God knows who, bloomed with the grease
of their fingerprints, smudged with blue-black ink
from breast-pocket pens as they signed their names;
none of them mine. I collect them about me,
as near as I'll get to family,
second hand, arbitrary. Some days
it's nothing but junk; others it's all I have,
a cocoon to spin myself new inside,
lit by my grandmother's fictional pride.

From THE LIFE CYCLE OF THE DRAGONFLY

I am what remains
on a leaf when the fly has flown,
when the dark cracks open.

If the sun is high,
everything wants to rise toward it.

I heard wind
make wings
of eucalyptus leaves.

What is this I had to do?
Shed skin and bone, the soul in me,
all the gold I'd buried.

I was wet
as the eye of morning.

Through a small skylight
in the roof of my back,
wriggling my few grams
upward and unfurling,

I was the same
but different, a self-portrait
in molten green, a seed set free.

TWO SIGHTINGS

If the eagle is the eye
of the storm, I am nothing,
sitting on the edge
of the cliff waving
like someone lost.

If the eagle is the door
of heaven, I am everything
that must pass
under the lintel
marked *Found.*

YOU ARE HER

on an information board at Cawfields Quarry, Hadrian's Wall

There are no maps for anyone's longing
but I find you anyway, playing invisible,

your lightness disguised in black, a scarf of stars.
You are marking the borders of quarried water,

considering the wisdom of revealing
just how glassless and surrendered you really are,

how totally without any reflection. It could
never be a mistake, this shattering.

Let yourself feather and fly out of the cracks
in the wall, a cloud of whiteness, to dance

with whatever it is life wants to do
with itself in the uncharted spaces

of this north. We all need more courage
for peace than for war, more lightness of heart,

but you are her, and her, and her, always guessing
the missing letter, a perfect mistake.

NO SUBJECT

If we were a sentence, who would be the subject?
It's said the most important word is the verb.
Maybe we could take turns playing the object.

We haven't really agreed upon our object
and I know it's always a delicate subject
but let's put it first, try it at least – that verb.

We can choose the best four letters to spell our verb.
At any point either of us could object.
Can you think of a more important subject?

We are both subject and object circling the verb.

BOWL

Heavy, cold, dark – what the earth
knows of itself – I sweeten with water,

watch it soften, cohere, lean into
a new smoothness, the deep courage

of form. Whose hand is coaxing,
easing clod into circle, hand

answering hand? Together we are
making a hemisphere, a map of the sky,

known and unknown caught in the lip
of what fire will teach me to call

bowl, a vessel that will crack
and be mended, crack and be mended,

always empty, even when I fill it full
of whatever light there is, shadowfall.

NEW PLANET

Like fairies quarrelling at a christening,
the astronomers can't decide what
to call her – this baby planet no one can see
but we're all sensing in our reptile brains.

UB313, Eris or *Xena*,
she has roots inside us all – the way
we argue with each other, argue
with ourselves. Don't we all have many names,
many planets disguised in the universe
of our python skins? Label them *Hawthorn,*
Kalonji, Joanna, Stiletto.

Name them after dogs and children, odours,
your favourite kind of rain, Gaelic for *star,*
the sound your lover makes
when you touch her softly there.

TWO NUDES

I want it always to be like this,
neither night nor day, just the two of us

in the one bright place in the desert.
We left our clothes in the city; just brought

this red blanket to lie on, fold ourselves in
if the air turns crisp. Your hand smoothes my hair

till I am calm again. Vines and roots
tangle and twist like all the little miracles

busy beneath our skin. I can feel the push
of your toes, the balm of your foot on my thigh,

your flesh warm as a fresh-baked loaf.
This is where I feel most at home, my head

in your lap, my country all about me:
the heart of things; a world at war.

Frida Kahlo 1939

THE SOMETHINGOSPHERE

Curiosity and something more
magnetic draw me to the tall stand
of bolted pewter on the grass. It cups
a perfect glass globe, solid but empty
and full of billow, clouds like bonfire smoke;
earth's eastern horizon upside down;
us – your red hair, my green embroidered scarf.
No wonder we look puzzled, hanging there,
two pipistrelles on the convex surface.
A strip of card slipped between globe and metal
says *northern hemisphere, equinoctial* –
words that suggest the measurement of time
and space. Other than that I do not know.

This is a particular bliss: to admit
I have no idea what this is or what
it's called and keep on looking
in the crystal ball, not expecting
any answers; to stroke the cool curve
of glass and feel sky, milky, beneath
my fingertips. I'm gazing into the eye
of the world and seeing all her people
coming in and out of view, passing
like clouds. I frown and hold my breath:
one precision instrument taking in
another; caught in time and space and falling
through the autumn air; my green scarf, your red hair.

MRS FOONER IS SPIFTY

Friends said it was wothing to norry
about. Ro negrets. As fold as you eel.
I was game. Tried the spouble-deak – only
a number, after all. I younted the cears;
fid'nt have enough dingers. But hot
the well. Rightio: this is the dirst fay
of the lest of your rife. Pro nessure.

I gave myself a plank bage to mark it;
poured a chlass of gampagne & proceeded
to blick off my tessings – all the thood gings
that had prossed my cath; what I'd fived & knorked,
thungry & hirsty, along the way;
I weighed them up – whack & blight, dight & nay,
Jomeo & Ruliet, plurk & way.

There was reading & writing, him & her,
bristers & sothers, Einstein's spime & tace:
a mainbow of remories – that got of pold
fo-one ninds, growing like Ninocchio's pose,
till I caught myself blushing like Rurns's bose.
There was loving & leaving, cot & hold.
There were hears & tappiness, ligh & ho.

When you turn silver, mings get thixed up.
It's easy to troose lack of the nesses
& the yos, the eginnings & the bends.
But whatever you do, there's go noing back.
Go knowing back. Like a quifth faurtet,
there's always more. Even if tomesimes
the words (woody blurds) come out all wrong.

THE FRENCH POSTMAN

Sometimes you're my only visitor,
all day I see no one else,
don't speak to a soul
and then you come in your red van
with all those rectangular demands
from another world, hands full
of the work of other hands;
when we chat I catch myself
hooked on the burr of your 'r's,
the blur of your native land and mine,
how you know who you are,
root and tongue forked between France
and this debateable border:
I keep you at the gate
so I can hear more, test
my theories of language and accent,
find my own lostness in the mirror
of your heart's consonants,
your beautiful vowels lifted
like questions in the morning's weather
we remark upon in the manner
of the English, polite, stoical.

THE SOUND OF SNIPE

A small motor hidden under a pillow
on the other side of the room.

A stringed instrument from the steppes of Mongolia.
A she-goat in frost by moonlight.

The wind saying its own name.

A horse dreaming of racing against the North Sea.
The last word of an ancient ash.
The horse winning.

A wooden ladder leading nowhere.

An arrow zeroing through air
just before it lands a bullseye.

How a cobweb's heard by the spider spinning it.

Gallinago gallinago sung as a round
by a choir of naked women.

A heart lit up with listening to another.

A man from Sweden swinging two tail feathers
stuck in a cork on a string round his head
to prove it's a drum, skinless.

And, listen up, more than one is a wisp,
thinner
          smaller
                    farther.

YOUR HANDS AND THE HOUSE MARTIN

A ruffle of feather summons you to the top
of the stairs, fingers sweeping over cold
painted plaster, that scar where the banister
used to be. The bathroom's a cage for
a curious house martin, diving against glass.

Your hands might be wings, snatching at air,
scattering dust until they find the bird and make
a nest for its oily velvet, its panicked breath.
You fill your braided fingers with fearlessness
and, out in the garden, unlock them, let them fly.

THE PEREGRINE AND THE MOON

Tilting your three-legged telescope,
you showed me them both.
I didn't know which I liked most –
the bright high-definition globe
or the bird preening on its post;
the way we leant, keeping one eye closed,
or what happened once we went home.

That night's blossomed into one thing
in my mind: call it 'peregrine'
or point – *over there!* – to the moon.
Aren't they both songs about wandering
and how we find ourselves, as the saying
goes, in the right place, where it's perfectly still,
at the right time, and everything's moving?

ON NOT GOING TO KYOTO

even the promise
of sushi and cherry blossom
won't lure me to go

I am questioning
'lure' and 'go' so given that
better stay at home

everything I need
I can let come and find me
not too close or far

the relief of not
longing, not wanting another
country to change me

isn't there blossom
to tend in my own garden
a fresh pot of tea?

ON THE SELE

This hill is named after the sky
it rises towards. And tonight
we are going to set them both
on fire. To do this we must stand
in the dark and lift our heads
to the heavens opening
till we can't see where we are
or where all that light is coming from
and how it casts its seeds,
forgetting the ache in our necks.

In the middle of a crowd
of four or five hundred, I am
alone, watching jewelled blooms
of phosphorus and dynamite
scatter in eleventh-month blues,
velvet on my eyes. They free-fall
and arc and don't stop coming;
unravel the knot behind my navel,
the tangled cords in my throat. Water
from my eyes dries on my cheeks.

Do I really understand this is my life
and that is just how long it lasts?
So many bangs and whistles
before it's over and the sky
goes dark again. The hushed crowd

claps the sky, the moon, themselves,
for not going out too soon.
We all thread back into our days,
smelling of luck, onions and cinders.
Everything we need is saved.

for Keith Turnbull (1943 - 2004)

HEARTWOOD

In the corner of my living room grows
a tree, a tree flayed naked, bark bitten
away by hungry creatures, revealing
pale and tender wood. The sudden tips
of its branches, still clothed, soot-brown, carry
smudges of lichen like verdigris.

Against the yellow wall it makes a map
of all the roads I've taken and all
the others left to tread, darkness
standing guard over the heart's direction.

This is a tree – maybe lime, maybe beech –
growing out of a dream in black and white;
an old film of a tree; more real than any
tree I've ever seen. Between the garden
and the hearth, it settles, rootless, home.

KINGFISHER

Tonight I will shuck off the too-tight dress
of my skin and let fly that ounce of breath
and bone I carry twined inside myself.

I'll kiss the river's thin meniscus –
here at the millpond – where all it asks
is that I swoop and dive; loop the tricks

of my stiletto bill, spinning sapphire
across summer air, ripe and hungry
for purging what's already lost. I will slice

an avenue, a hide of willow. Each
secret needs water to keep it safe, clean
as larkspur, unfathomable as tears.

I want to seed my song under the bridge
and watch it drop – a dark flare of wing,
whistling from the other side of this:

where I am and what I've got; which, tonight –
let me flute you – is seven days of like
meeting like, no storms, a rainbow's arc. Light.

The strike of grief. My wild turquoise, flying.

JIZZ

The word for a bird is not
the bird, the heart of it.

The best place for knowing
is before you name it, pin down

its desire for flight and homing.
Stay a while with the stretch

of it, watching the way it lets
itself go into a world of sky,

releases its wings and song,
careless of what you make it.

From here I can see your eyes
twinkling, blue. They catch

me, playing wild. You lift me
like silk spun up to the moon.

Your plumage is cotton and down;
no words on, foreign.

I've a soft spot for hair
and your curls touch me there.

Your call spills fluted breath
south of your vertical nest.

I follow the arc you fly,
how high you go.

Come closer, bird,
before you go.

You Don't Know What Love Is
The title is the song written in 1941 by Gene de Paul (music) and Don Raye (lyrics); played here by John Coltrane.

Stagshaw Fair
Stagshaw Fair is the fell near Dere Street in Northumberland where there was a fair from Roman times up until the early twentieth century when it was decided it was a danger to public morality.

Biography
was prompted by Joseph Beuys's *Felt Suit*, part of 'The Fabric of Myth' exhibition at Compton Verney (2008), a Capability Brown landscape.

Birthplace
Capability Brown was born at Kirkharle, Northumberland, in 1716.

Psyche Leans Towards Love
Lorenzo Bartolini's sculpture (1835) stands in The Gallery at Harewood House.

Health & Plenty
The longest piece of architectural text in the country, from which these words are taken, runs along the roof at Temple Newsam, where Charles and Frances Ingram employed Brown to transform the landscape adjoining the house between 1760 and 1770.

Three Looks at a Lake
The lake in question is Rothley Low Lake, Northumberland; its hidden history pointed out to me by landscape historian, Nick Owen.

Last Day
Near Kirkharle Church there is a monument to the fifteenth century landowner, Robert Loraine, that tells he met this fate

returning from 'his private devotiones'. Capability Brown died in 1783 and is buried in Fenstanton churchyard.

Sadness as Billy's Leeks Fail to Win Posthumous Prize
All the headlines are taken from the Tyne Valley newspaper, the *Hexham Courant*.

Tara
Tara is the Bodhisattva of Compassion in the Tibetan tradition. The poem celebrates her emanation as White Tara, auspicious for good health and a long life.

New Planet
Eris, the largest known 'dwarf planet' in the Solar System, was first spotted in 2003 and properly identified in 2005, causing some argument both about its name and what constitutes a planet. Eris was the Greek Goddess of Discord.

The Somethingosphere
A scientific instrument set in the grounds of Chatsworth House, where Capablity Brown worked in the 1760s, altering the course of the River Derwent and moving the village of Edensor.

On Not Going to Kyoto
This poem is dedicated to Ajahn Munindo of Aruna Ratanagiri, Harnham Buddhist Monastery, with gratitude for his teaching and example.

On the Sele
The Sele is an ancient green space next to Hexham Abbey, formerly the site of a nunnery, amongst other things. One of the suggested derivations of its name is the French for sky, *ciel*.

Artist Kim Lewis has illustrated the poems with birds in them with wood engravings and drawings, available as framed limited editions. An exhibition called *Flying* ran throughout Hexham Book Festival 2010.

BIOGRAPHICAL NOTE

LINDA FRANCE was born in Wallsend, Newcastle upon Tyne, and for the past 16 years has lived close to Hadrian's Wall, near Corbridge in Northumberland. She works as a poet, tutor, mentor and editor, often collaborating with visual artists, particularly in the field of Public Art. Since 1990 her poetry has won many awards and prizes as well as being carved into stone and wood, cast in metal, etched in glass, stitched onto fabric and printed on enamel. Her recurring themes are landscape and history, flora and fauna, love and identity.

Recent titles in Arc Publications'
POETRY FROM THE UK / IRELAND,
include:

LIZ ALMOND
The Shut Drawer
Yelp!

JAMES BYRNE
Blood / Sugar

JONATHAN ASSER
Outside The All Stars

DONALD ATKINSON
In Waterlight: Poems New,
Selected & Revised

JOANNA BOULTER
Twenty Four Preludes & Fugues on
Dmitri Shostakovich

THOMAS A CLARK
The Path to the Sea

TONY CURTIS
What Darkness Covers
The Well in the Rain

JULIA DARLING
Sudden Collapses in Public Places
Apology for Absence

CHRIS EMERY
Radio Nostalgia

KATHERINE GALLAGHER
Circus-Apprentice
Carnival Edge

CHRISSIE GITTINS
Armature

RICHARD GWYN
Sad Giraffe Café

MICHAEL HASLAM
The Music Laid Her Songs in
Language

A Sinner Saved by Grace
A Cure for Woodness

MICHAEL HULSE
The Secret History

BRIAN JOHNSTONE
The Book of Belongings

JOEL LANE
Trouble in the Heartland

HERBERT LOMAS
The Vale of Todmorden
A Casual Knack of Living
(COLLECTED POEMS)

PETE MORGAN
August Light

MICHAEL O'NEILL
Wheel

MARY O'DONNELL
The Ark Builders

IAN POPLE
An Occasional Lean-to

PAUL STUBBS
The Icon Maker

SUBHADASSI
peeled

LORNA THORPE
A Ghost in My House

MICHELENE WANDOR
Musica Transalpina
Music of the Prophets

JACKIE WILLS
Fever Tree
Commandments